KT-562-187

WHAT'S INSIDE?

SHELLS

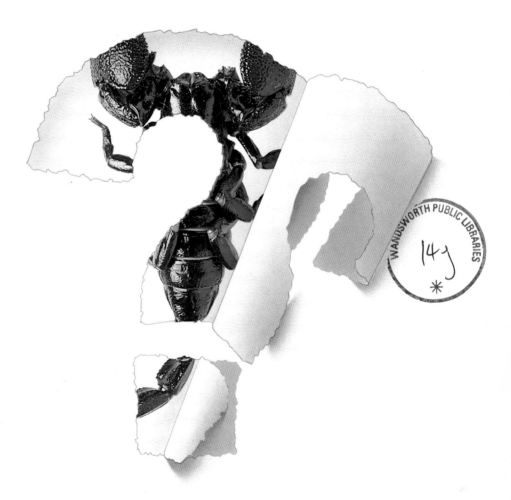

WANDSWORTH PUBLIC LIBRARIES

14j

DORLING KINDERSLEY
LONDON • NEW YORK • STUTTGART

300 487 101   J595.3 Roys   8194

SNAIL

All snails are damp and slimy. They move very slowly,
munching leaves as they go. In winter they curl up
inside their shells and sleep until spring.

The snail's eyes are at the end
of these two long stalks.

He uses these
two short feelers
for tasting and
touching things.

The shell is coiled
in a spiral shape.
As the snail grows
its shell gets bigger too.

He doesn't have legs, just a single foot
that slides along on a layer of gooey slime

The snail has a rough tongue that works like a cheese grater. It scrapes off tasty bits of leaf to eat.

This is his heart.

This space is called the mantle. It is where his head goes when he disappears inside his shell.

His kidneys help make his slime slimier.

Slime comes out here.

His stomach breaks his food down to mush; eventually that mush becomes slime.

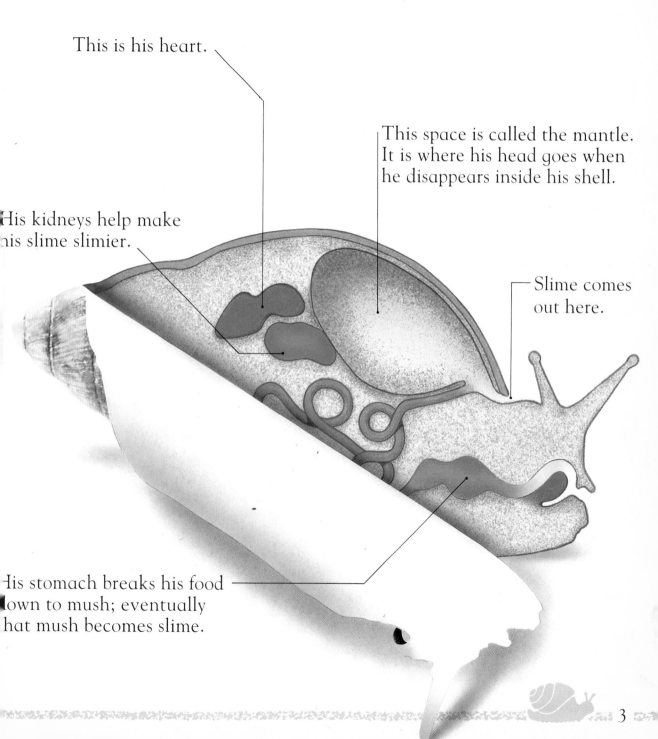

OYSTER

Oysters are shellfish that live in the sea.
They bury themselves in sand or mud, or attach
themselves to rocks. They feed on tiny plants
and animals in the water that swirls around them.

The oyster's shell
is very hard.

As the oyster grow
inside, the shell
grows too, adding
extra rings like
a tree trunk.

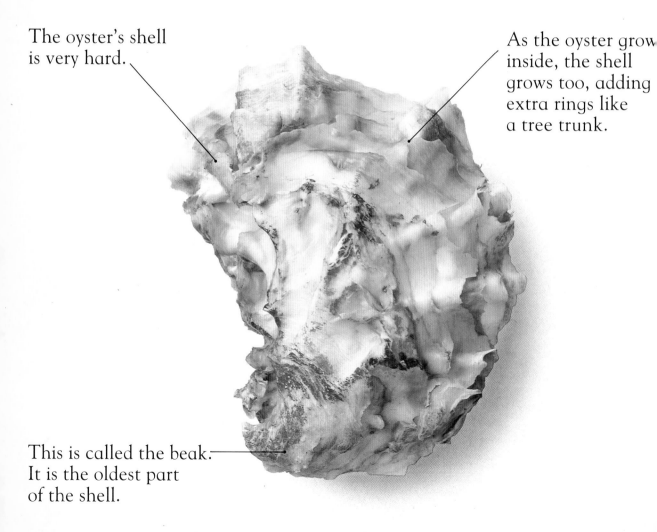

This is called the beak.
It is the oldest part
of the shell.

The oyster opens its shell just enough to let water wash through. Little hairs trap tiny plants and animals, and pass them along to the oyster's mouth.

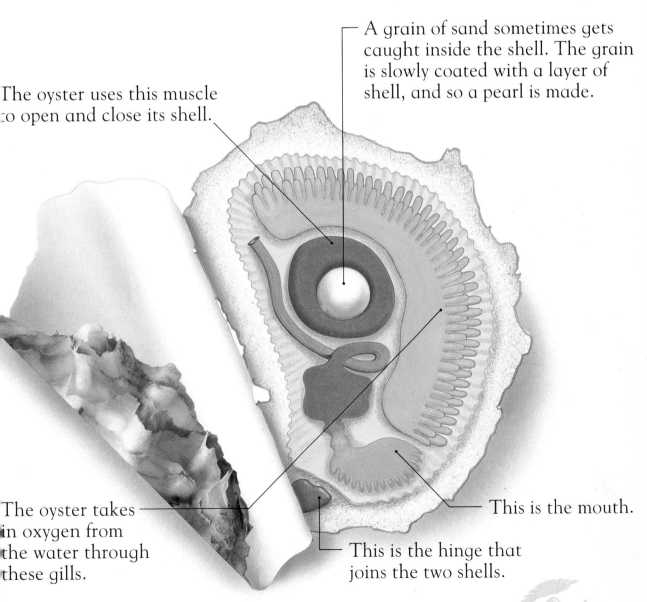

A grain of sand sometimes gets caught inside the shell. The grain is slowly coated with a layer of shell, and so a pearl is made.

The oyster uses this muscle to open and close its shell.

This is the mouth.

The oyster takes in oxygen from the water through these gills.

This is the hinge that joins the two shells.

TORTOISE

This tortoise has an armoured shell just like a tank.
It protects his body. When he is frightened he pulls his head and
legs inside his shell and waits until it is safe to come out again.

He moves along slowly
because his shell is so heavy.

He eats slugs and snails
and worms and leaves.
He has a horny beak,
like a bird, and no teeth

These strong claws help
the tortoise to burrow into
the ground to make a nest.

His legs are covered with
folds of thick scaly skin.

The tortoise has a long neck so he can poke his head out of his shell and look around.

This is his backbone. He cannot move it because it is fixed to his shell.

This is the tortoise's heart.

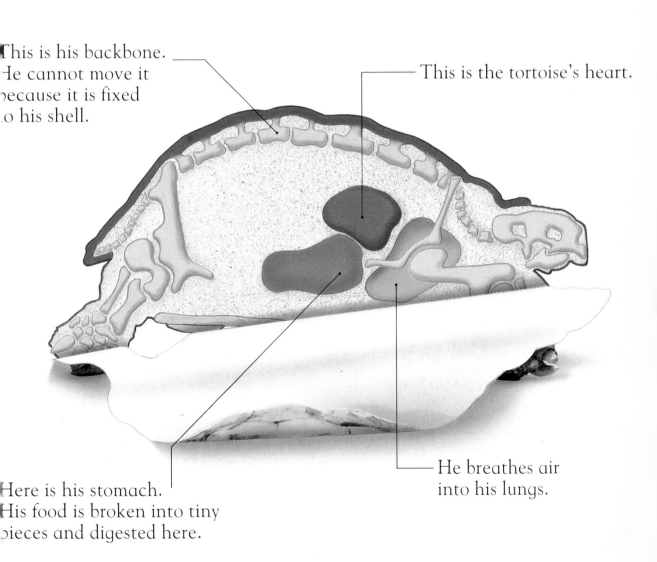

Here is his stomach. His food is broken into tiny pieces and digested here.

He breathes air into his lungs.

CRAB

Crabs live in the sea, near the shore. You may have seen
some scuttling about on the beach at low tide looking for food.

These powerful pincers are used
for swimming as well as for holding
food and nipping toes!

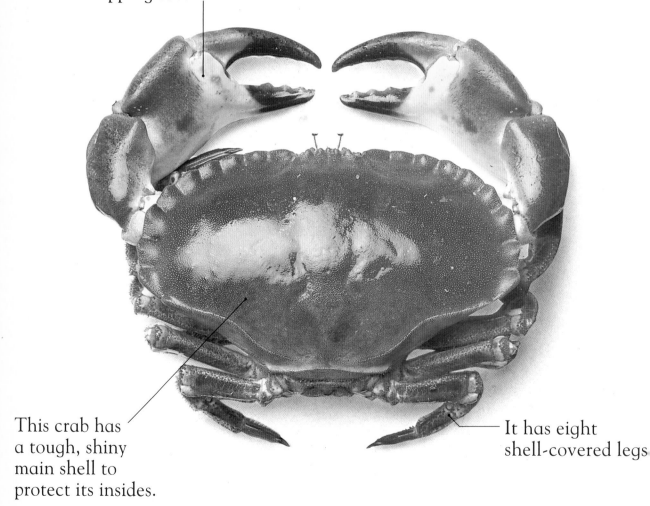

This crab has
a tough, shiny
main shell to
protect its insides.

It has eight
shell-covered legs.

Crabs move sideways, not forwards or backwards. They can run quite fast and some crabs can run up cliffs or even trees.

These strong muscles open and close its pincers.

The crab's tiny eyes are on the end of these stalks.

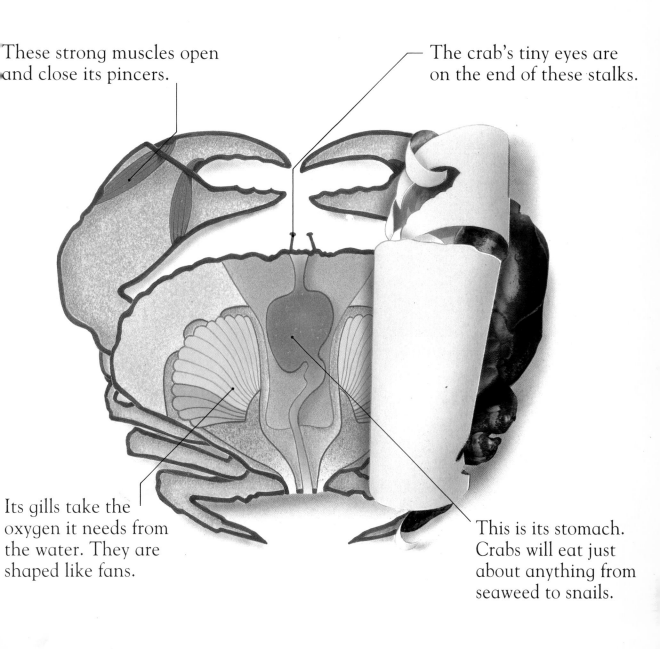

Its gills take the oxygen it needs from the water. They are shaped like fans.

This is its stomach. Crabs will eat just about anything from seaweed to snails.

SCORPION

Scorpions have an unusual weapon – a poisonous sting in the tip of their tails. Their poison kills insects and some scorpions could kill a person.

The scorpion uses these large pincers for catching and grasping food.

The scorpion has a sharp sting in its tail. It uses this to defend itself and to kill animals too big to kill with its claws.

Its shell is completely waterproof. This stops the scorpion's moist insides from drying out.

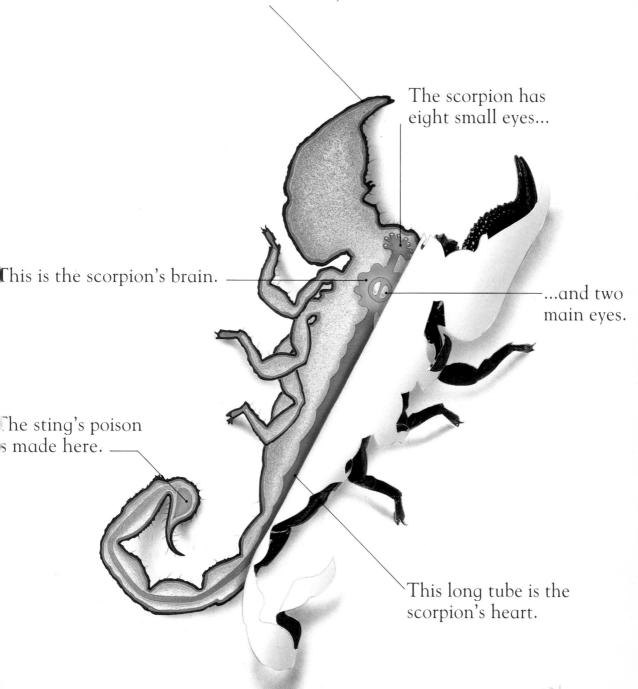

Underneath this shell a new shell is growing. When the scorpion grows too big for the old shell, it will burst out of it.

The scorpion has eight small eyes...

This is the scorpion's brain.

...and two main eyes.

The sting's poison is made here.

This long tube is the scorpion's heart.

NAUTILUS

The nautilus belongs to the same family as the octopus.
It lives at the bottom of deep tropical seas. Ancient nautiluses
were among the earliest animals to appear on earth,
hundreds of millions of years ago.

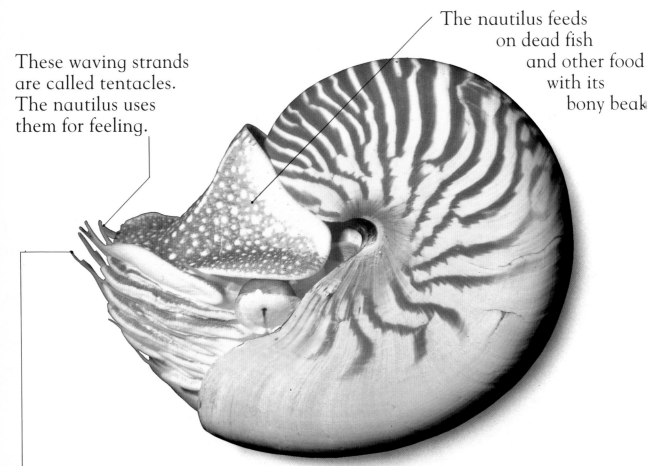

These waving strands
are called tentacles.
The nautilus uses
them for feeling.

The nautilus feeds
on dead fish
and other food
with its
bony beak

The tip of each tentacle has
ridges of rough skin so it can
cling to stones and shells.

The nautilus swims backwards b
sucking water into its body
then shooting it out.

The nautilus starts life in a tiny shell. As it grows it adds a new and bigger compartment to its shell and moves into it.

Under its beak the nautilus has a mouth with a tongue and teeth.

The empty compartments are filled with water and gas to help the nautilus move up and down in the sea.

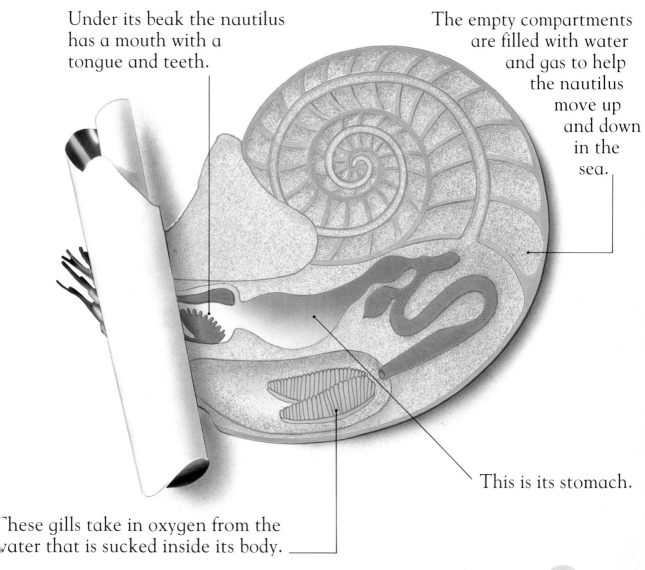

This is its stomach.

These gills take in oxygen from the water that is sucked inside its body.

SEA URCHIN

Sea urchins live on rocky seashores or in rock pools.
They look like harmless plants swaying in the water, but they are
covered with sharp spines, so be careful not to step on one!

Sharp spines defend the
sea urchin from its enemies.

The sea urchin
moves across the
rocks on tube-
shaped feet.

Each foot has a sucker
on the end. The sucker
helps the sea urchin to
cling to the rocks.

The sea urchin's mouth is on the underside of its body, facing the sea bed.

The spines grow out of these bumps.

Waste food leaves the body here.

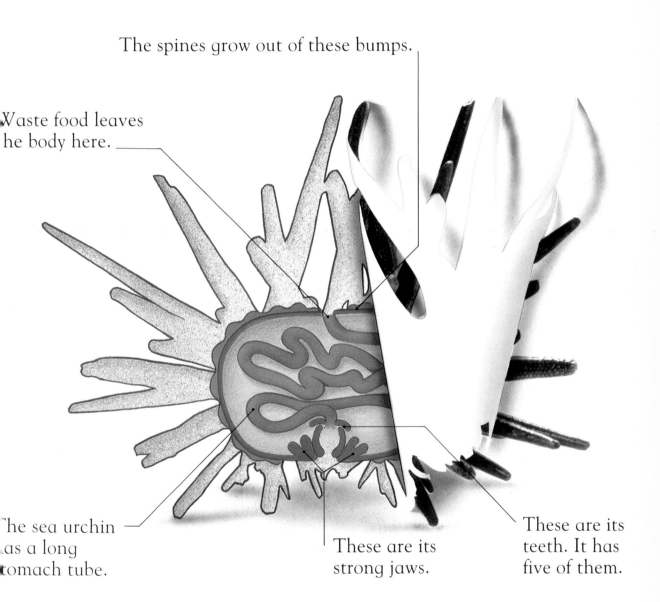

The sea urchin has a long stomach tube.

These are its strong jaws.

These are its teeth. It has five of them.

HERMIT CRAB

The hermit crab does not live in its own shell. Instead
it moves into the empty shell of another sea creature.
When it grows too big for its borrowed home,
the crab looks for a larger shell and scuttles into it.

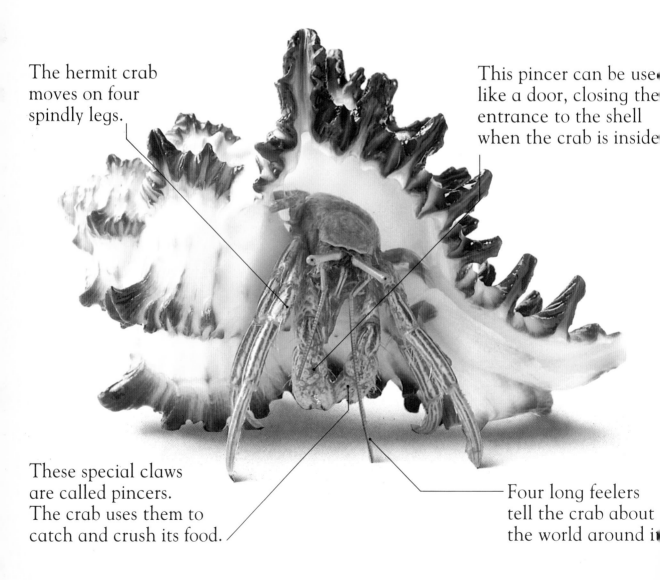

The hermit crab
moves on four
spindly legs.

This pincer can be use
like a door, closing the
entrance to the shell
when the crab is inside

These special claws
are called pincers.
The crab uses them to
catch and crush its food.

Four long feelers
tell the crab about
the world around i

This hermit crab is living in an abandoned murex shell. Its body is soft, and without the shell it would be completely unprotected.

The shell has lots of separate compartments. The hermit crab curls up to ~~sit~~ in one of the chambers.

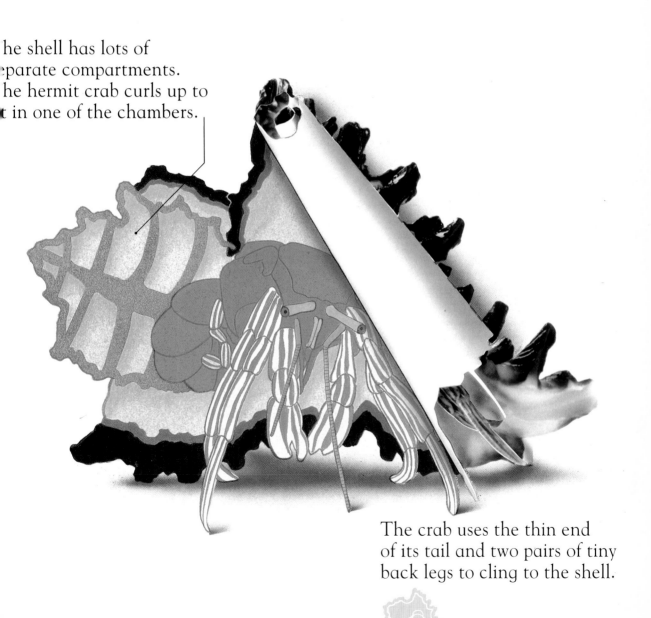

The crab uses the thin end of its tail and two pairs of tiny back legs to cling to the shell.

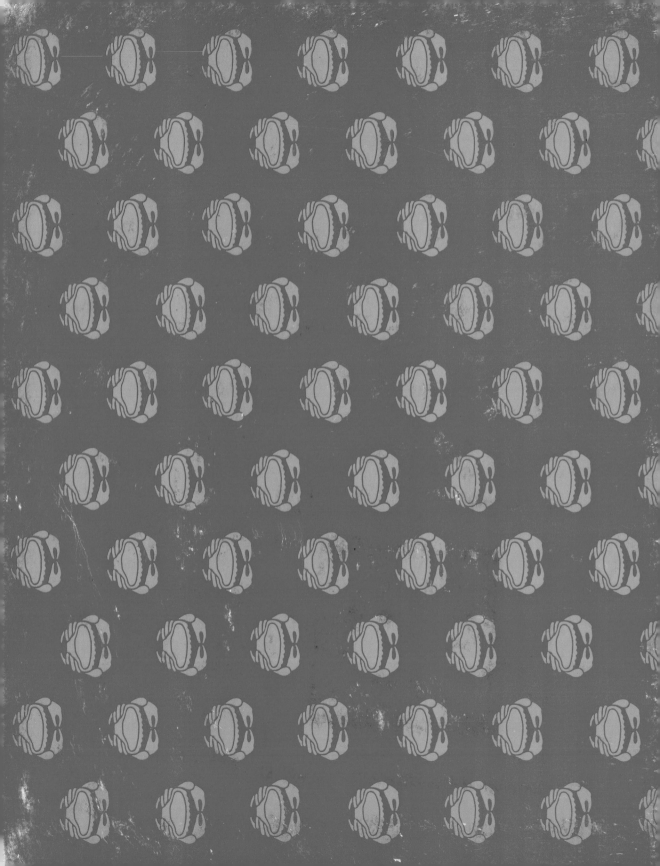